IRELAND

A TRUE BOOK

by

Brendan January

Children's Press®

A Division of Grolier Publishing

New York London Hong Kong Sydney
Danbury, Connecticut

A young Irish girl

Reading Consultant
Linda Cornwell
Learning Resource Consultant
Indiana Department of
Education

Author's Dedication:
To the memory of
Mary O'Brien Curran

Visit Children's Press® on the
Internet at:
http://publishing.grolier.com

Library of Congress Cataloging-in-Publication Data

January, Brendan, 1972–
    Ireland / by Brendan January.
        p.   cm.   —   (A true book)
    Summary: Presents an overview of the history, geography, climate, and
culture of Ireland.
    ISBN: 0-516-21186-2 (lib. bdg.)   0-516-26493-1 (pbk.)
    1. Ireland—Juvenile literature.   [1. Ireland.]   I. Title.   II. Series.
DA906.J28   1999
941.5—dc21   98-15762
                                                                                        CIP
                                                                                        AC

GROLIER
PUBLISHING

Contents

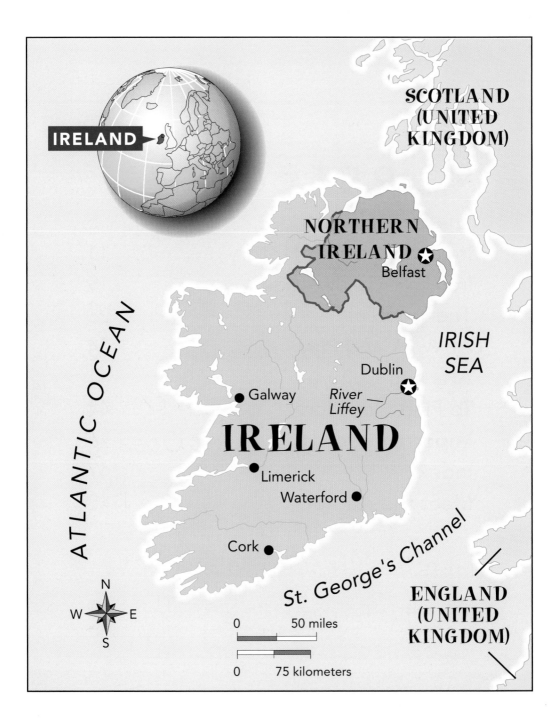

SCOTLAND
(UNITED
KINGDOM)

NORTHERN
IRELAND ✪
Belfast

IRISH
SEA

ATLANTIC OCEAN

Galway

Dublin ★
River
Liffey

IRELAND

Limerick
Waterford

Cork

St. George's Channel

ENGLAND
(UNITED
KINGDOM)

N
W E
S

0   50 miles

0   75 kilometers

The Emerald Island

Ireland is a small island located northwest of Europe. On three sides, Ireland faces the chilly waters of the Atlantic Ocean. The fourth side borders the Irish Sea. Because Ireland is almost surrounded by ocean, its climate is very wet. The ocean's currents constantly

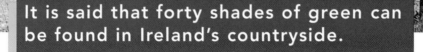
It is said that forty shades of green can be found in Ireland's countryside.

move warm, moist air across the island. Showers often drench Ireland with mist and rain.

The damp weather is not all bad, however. The frequent

rainstorms give Ireland's grass a lush, dark-green color. Ireland's landscape is covered with spectacular patches of green fields. A poet called Ireland the "emerald of Europe." An emerald is a beautiful green jewel.

Several mountain ranges run along the outer edges of the island. In Ireland's center lie swampy areas called bogs. Gently rolling hills of farmland are also found here. The Irish

Cows graze on Ireland's lush farmland.

use this area mostly to raise cattle, sheep, and horses.

Along the western edge of Ireland, the Atlantic Ocean's waves pound against the shoreline. This has left the coast jagged and rocky with steep cliffs. Some of them rise hundreds of feet straight up from the water.

The Cliffs of Moher are located in western Ireland's County Clare.

To Ireland's east lies a larger island—Great Britain. Great Britain is divided into England, Wales, Scotland, and Northern Ireland. Scotland is only 13 miles (21 kilometers) from Ireland's northeastern coast. Thousands of years ago, the first humans arrived in Ireland on these shores.

Ireland's Ancient History

More than eight thousand years ago, hunters came to Ireland from Scotland. They quickly spread out over the island. Four thousand years later, a new group of settlers arrived. These settlers farmed and raised animals. They were

A visitor explores the ruins at Newgrange.

also expert builders. Today, at places such as Newgrange, their ancient tombs still rise above the Irish landscape.

Around 500 B.C., the Celts (KELTS) arrived on Ireland's shores from Britain and Europe. The Celts were talented crafts-men and brave warriors. They conquered Ireland and divided it into small kingdoms.

Ancient Celts, whose influence can still be found throughout Ireland

Celtic laws and traditions ruled Ireland. The Celtic language, called Gaelic (GAY-lik), later became the Irish language. The Celts developed a rich tradition of myths and storytelling. Many Celtic characters survive today in Irish stories. (One character, the leprechaun, is a mischievous fairy who will do anything to protect his pot of gold.) Hundreds of years after arriving in Ireland,

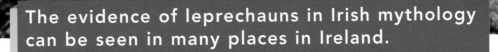

The evidence of leprechauns in Irish mythology can be seen in many places in Ireland.

the Celts mixed and married with the original settlers, creating the Irish people.

In the 300s and 400s, the Irish often raided towns in Scotland and England. On one raid, they captured a sixteen-year-old boy and brought him back to Ireland as a slave. The boy later escaped. In A.D. 432, he returned to Ireland with a new religion—Christianity. He is now known as Saint Patrick.

St. Patrick taught Christianity to the Irish. According to legend, some listeners asked St. Patrick about the Christian idea of one God as the Father, the Son, and the Holy Spirit. St. Patrick picked a shamrock from the grass. He explained that it has three leaves, but it

St. Patrick (left) is the patron saint of Ireland. (A patron saint is a saint who is believed to look after a particular country.) The shamrock (above) is the national symbol of Ireland.

is also one plant. Since then, the shamrock has become Ireland's national flower.

When St. Patrick died in A.D. 465, Christianity had spread through Ireland. Today, St. Patrick is the most honored of Ireland's saints. Every year on March 17, people around the world join the Irish to celebrate St. Patrick's Day.

Ireland's Golden Age

Many Christian holy men, called monks, lived in Ireland. These monks gathered together in religious communities called monasteries. They carefully copied by hand ancient works of literature and the Bible. In the late 400s and 500s, the system of law and

This illustration of a monk at work also happens to be the first known picture of a man wearing glasses.

order in Europe collapsed. However, Ireland was left out of these problems. Safe in

ETSYRIAM SOBAL · ETCONVERTIT
IOAB · ET PERCYSSIT EDOM INVAL
LE SALINARVM · XII MILIA ·

A page from
a book of
Psalms that
was created
in about 750.

their monasteries, Irish monks
continued to copy rare written
works. Other monks crafted
religious objects made from silver, gold, and sparkling jewels.

The Book of Kells

▲An illustration of Saint Mark from the Book of Kells

The Book of Kells was created by monks in the 700s and 800s. It contains sections of the Gospels of the New Testament. The Book of Kells is considered to be one of the greatest masterpieces of Irish art. Each page is covered with intricate decorations and designs. Today, the Book of Kells is on display at Trinity College in Dublin.

◄ This page shows some of the fine art contained in the Book of Kells.

Around 800, new invaders—
the Vikings—came to Ireland
from northern Europe. They
attacked the monasteries and
stole the precious gold, silver,
and jewels.

Vikings sailed
to Ireland's
shores on
ships that
were similar
to this one.

These remains of a monastery tower are located in Killarney, in southwestern Ireland.

Many monasteries were built with giant stone towers. When a Viking ship was spotted, the monks locked themselves inside for safety. Today, many of these towers still dot the Irish countryside.

Throughout the 800s and 900s, many Vikings settled in Ireland and built towns. Ireland's capital city, Dublin, was founded by Vikings. In 1014, the Irish king Brian Boru led an Irish army against the Vikings. After a bloody battle at Clontarf, just outside Dublin, the Vikings' power in Ireland ended.

The Troubles

During the 1500s, Christians in Europe split into two groups— the Protestants and the Catholics. The Protestants rebelled against the Catholics and their leader, the pope. The Europeans suffered through several bloody religious wars. Eventually, the conflict came to Ireland.

King Henry VIII ruled England from 1509 to 1547.

The English had been coming to Ireland since the 1200s. Sometimes they conquered parts of Ireland. Other times, they settled peacefully. In 1534, the English king, Henry VIII,

This painting illustrates the removal of Irish Catholics from their land.

decided to make England and Ireland Protestant. The Irish people, however, wanted to remain Catholic. In response, Henry sent soldiers to take over the island. They drove the Irish off their land and gave it to Protestant leaders.

During the next three hundred fifty years, the Irish tried many times to win their freedom from England. But they were always defeated. In 1916, Irish rebels seized important buildings in Dublin. Soon England and Ireland were at war. After several years, a

A view of a section of Dublin after the Irish Rebellion of 1916.

peace treaty was signed. The Irish could finally rule themselves.

However, many people living in the northern part of Ireland were Protestant. They did not want to join Catholic Ireland. In 1920, they decided to remain a part of Great Britain called Northern Ireland. Today, the island is still divided into two countries.

For many years, Catholics and Protestants in Northern Ireland have fought each other. Many

Citizens look over the damage after a night of fighting between Protestants and Catholics in West Belfast, Northern Ireland, in 1997.

people have been killed or injured. The Irish call these events "the Troubles." Today, meetings are taking place between the leaders of Ireland and Great Britain. The Irish hope the Troubles will end soon.

Ireland's flag

The flag of Ireland was created in the mid-1800s. The orange color represents the Protestants in Ireland. The green color represents the Catholics. The white stripe represents the hope for peace between the two groups.

The Irish Potato Famine

In this 1847 illustration, starving Irish try to get inside a workhouse, which is similar to a soup kitchen, for a meal.

For years, Ireland's major crop was potatoes. But in 1845–47, the potato crops failed. Thousands of Irish starved. These years became known as the Great Hunger, or the Irish Potato Famine. As a result, millions of Irish fled from their homeland to North America or Australia. In just a few years, Ireland's population fell from 8 million to 5 million.

At Work and Play

For hundreds of years, most Irish have lived and worked in the countryside. But today, only one of every five Irish still works on farms. Many work in factories, and almost half of the population lives in cities.

Dublin and Cork are Ireland's biggest cities. Dublin

Present-day farmers build a haystack on a farm in north-western Ireland (left). This worker (above) is preparing airplane parts in a factory in Northern Ireland.

sits on the River Liffey on Ireland's eastern coast. It is the cultural and political capital of Ireland. Cork is located on Ireland's southern coast. Cork

An aerial view of Dublin and the River Liffey (above), A typical street in Cork, Ireland's second-largest city (right)

is a manufacturing center and the second-largest city in Ireland. Galway, Limerick, and Waterford are other important Irish cities.

Tourism is an important industry in Ireland. Each year, millions

Visitors tour Johnstown Castle, located in southeastern Ireland (above). This Irishman (right) works at Bunratty Castle and Folk Park, another popular site for visitors.

of visitors travel to Ireland to view its beautiful scenery. There, they enjoy one of the cleanest environments in the world. Visitors also come to experience the warmth and humor of Ireland's people.

37

The Irish enjoy rough-and-tumble games. Hurling is an ancient Irish sport. There are fifteen players on each team. Each player carries a stick called a hurley. Using the hurley, the players try to knock a small leather ball through two goalposts. The games are fast, exciting, and attract thousands of fans.

Gaelic football looks like a mix of rugby and soccer. Like hurling, each team has fifteen members. The players try to kick a leather ball between two tall

The sport of hurling (above) was first mentioned in Celtic myths. A Gaelic football game between Ireland and New Zealand (right)

uprights or into a goal. Gaelic football is full of fast, hard-hitting movement.

The Irish also enjoy more peaceful sports, such as horse racing. The Irish Derby

Horses and spectators prepare for the Irish Grand National (above). Irish fans at a World Cup soccer match (right)

and the Irish Grand National are the most famous races.

Soccer is also extremely popular in Ireland. When the Irish national soccer team plays in the World Cup, stores close and businesses shut down so everyone can watch.

Arts and Culture

Despite Ireland's small size, it has produced a remarkable number of world-famous writers, poets, and musicians. The tradition of Irish writing and music began two thousand years ago with the Celts.

Almost three hundred years ago, Jonathan Swift wrote

Folk musicians (left) and shows featuring folk dancing (right) are common throughout Ireland.

about Gulliver, who had many adventures in *Gulliver's Travels.* William B. Yeats and James Joyce are also famous writers.

Today, many Irish artists enjoy enormous popularity.

The rock band U2 and dance groups such as Riverdance have millions of fans. Other artists, such as the Chieftains, will continue to bring the music and culture of the Emerald Island to audiences throughout the world.

Young musicians on a Dublin street

To Find Out More

Here are some additional resources to help you learn more about the nation of Ireland:

Books

A Day in the Life of Ireland. Collins Publishers, 1991.

Bailey, Donna and Anna Sproule. **Ireland.** Raintree Steck-Vaughn, 1990.

Gerard-Sharp, Lisa and Tim Perry. **Ireland.** Dorling Kindersley, 1995.

Gibbons, Gail. **St. Patrick's Day.** Holiday House, 1995.

Kent, Deborah. **Dublin.** Children's Press, 1997.

Organizations and Online Sites

Irish American Cultural Association (IACA)
10415 S. Western
Chicago, IL 60643

Irish Genealogical Foundation (IGF)
P.O. Box 7575
Kansas City, MO 64116

If your family came from Ireland, this group can help you find information about your Irish relatives.

Irish Literature, Folklore, and Drama
http://www.luminarium.org/mythology/ireland/

This site has lists of Irish myths and heroes. It also includes links to sites about Irish history, current events, food, and more.

Irish Music on the Web
http://www.bess.tcd.ie/music.htm

Enjoy everything from Celtic music to modern favorites, along with the Irish national anthem in both Gaelic and English.

Important Words

climate the usual weather in a certain place

culture the way of life, ideas, customs, and traditions of a particular group of people

famine period of time when there is not enough food for people to eat

intricate detailed and complicated

rare uncommon, not often seen

tradition the passing on of customs, ideas, and beliefs from one generation to the next

Index

Meet the Author

Brendan January was born and raised in Pleasantville, New York. He earned his B.A. in history and English at Haverford College and an M.A. in Journalism from Columbia University. This is Mr. January's seventh book for Children's Press.